Contents

1.
2.
3.
   a.
4.
   a.
5.
   a.
   b.
6.
   a.
   b.
   c.
7.
   a.
   b.
   c.
8.
   a.
   b.
   c.
9.
   a.
   b.
   c.

10.

     a.

     b.

     c.

11.

     a.

     b.

12.

     a.

13.

To my family.

TABLE OF CONTENTS

PART ONE

IN THE BUSTLING city of New Harbor, enterprising businesswoman Sophia Chen faces a daunting challenge when her company, Horizon Dynamics, teeters on the edge of bankruptcy. After losing a major private sector contract, Sophia decides to chart a new course by focusing on securing lucrative government contracts to revive her business.

Despite her determination, Sophia encounters a steep learning curve in navigating the complex world of government procurement. Recognizing the need for guidance, she forms an unexpected partnership with a retired government procurement specialist, William Hayes. Initially hesitant to mentor Sophia, William is drawn to her tenacity and eventually agrees to lend his expertise.

Together, Sophia and William embark on an arduous journey to decipher the intricate processes of bidding, compliance, and bureaucracy. They face fierce competition, ethical dilemmas, and hidden agendas within government agencies, all while striving to decode the language of Requests for Proposals (RFPs) and craft winning bids.

As they delve deeper into the world of government contracting, Sophia and William devise innovative strategies, leverage technology, and forge strategic alliances to bolster Horizon Dynamics' chances of success. Their efforts culminate in a high-stakes bid for a transformative government contract that could redefine the company's future.

"The Contract Conquest" offers a captivating narrative, blending business strategy, mentorship, and resilience. Through Sophia's determination and William's guidance, readers glean invaluable insights and practical advice on positioning their businesses for success in the competitive realm of government contracting.

Will Sophia and Horizon Dynamics secure the coveted government contract, or will unforeseen challenges thwart their ambitions? Join them on this compelling journey filled with twists, lessons, and the triumph of perseverance in the pursuit of entrepreneurial triumph.

PART TWO

THE MORNING SUN peeked through the office blinds, casting long shadows across Sophia Chen's desk cluttered with stacks of paperwork and faded post-it notes. She sat there, a whirlwind of determination masked behind a facade of serene composure. Sophia, the founder of Horizon Dynamics, was not one to yield easily, especially when her company stood on the precipice of ruin.

New Harbor, a city teeming with ambition and resilience, had been the canvas for Sophia's entrepreneurial dreams. Yet, the recent loss of a crucial private sector contract had left Horizon Dynamics adrift in a sea of uncertainty. The looming threat of financial demise weighed heavily on her shoulders as she mulled over the company's next move.

Sophia's gaze drifted toward the corner of her cluttered office, where a framed photo captured a moment frozen in time—a jubilant celebration marking the successful launch of Horizon Dynamics. That triumph felt like a distant memory now, a testament to the ephemeral nature of success in the volatile world of business.

With a sigh, Sophia made a bold decision—a pivot that could either resurrect her company or plunge it deeper into despair. Government contracts. A realm shrouded in mystery and complexity, yet brimming with potential. It was an audacious shift, a leap into uncharted territory.

As she delved into research, Sophia realized the daunting challenges that lay ahead. The convoluted jargon of Requests for Proposals (RFPs) seemed like an encrypted code, and navigating the labyrinthine landscape of government regulations felt like traversing an untamed wilderness.

A knock on the door disrupted her thoughts. "Come in," she called out, and in walked William Hayes, a retired government procurement specialist. His graying hair and wise, weathered eyes exuded experience—a man who'd weathered the storms of countless bidding wars and bureaucratic skirmishes.

"Ms. Chen," William began, his voice carrying a blend of wisdom and warmth, "I've heard of your endeavors into government contracts. You're swimming in murky waters, but I might have a life raft for you."

Sophia regarded him with a mix of curiosity and guarded hope. She hadn't expected assistance, especially not from someone with William's background. Yet, in that moment, she sensed a potential ally—a guide who could help her navigate the treacherous seas of government procurement.

And so, an unlikely partnership was forged—a bond between an embattled entrepreneur and a retired expert, each carrying their burdens and aspirations. Together, they would embark on a journey fraught with challenges, revelations, and the tantalizing promise of a transformative contract that could breathe new life into Horizon Dynamics.

The stage was set, the players assembled, as Sophia and William prepared to unravel the secrets and conquer the elusive realm of government procurement. Their journey toward the contract conquest had just begun.

PART THREE

SCENE 1

THE COFFEE MACHINE whirred to life in the small break room adjacent to Sophia's office. She watched as William expertly maneuvered the intricate mechanisms, a skill honed over years of brewing and bargaining, she presumed.

"Care for a cup?" William asked, his gaze fixed on the machine as he deftly adjusted the settings.

"Sure, thank you," Sophia replied, her mind still grappling with the enormity of the endeavor ahead.

As William poured the steaming brew into two mugs, Sophia couldn't help but feel a blend of trepidation and determination coursing through her veins. She stepped into the break room, taking in the faint aroma of freshly ground coffee intermingled with the faint scent of printer ink lingering on her fingertips.

"Ms. Chen," William began, handing her a mug, "I've seen many entrepreneurs venture into the realm of government contracts with stars in their eyes, only to falter amidst the bureaucracy. It's not for the faint of heart."

Sophia cradled the warm mug in her hands, her gaze meeting William's steady stare. "I understand it's a challenging landscape. But I can't let Horizon Dynamics fade into obscurity. I need to explore every avenue."

"Optimism and determination," William mused, a faint smile gracing his lips. "Two essential traits. But you'll need more than that. Strategy, foresight, and adaptability are key to navigating these waters."

The gravity of his words settled over Sophia. "I'm willing to learn. To adapt. I just don't want to make costly mistakes."

William nodded, acknowledging her concern. "Indeed. Mistakes can be expensive in this arena. That's why I've come here today—to offer guidance, share insights, and help you understand the nuances."

Sophia took a sip of her coffee, the warmth seeping into her as she absorbed William's words. "I appreciate your willingness to help, Mr. Hayes. Where do we start?"

With a twinkle in his eye, William set his mug down and reached for a folder tucked under his arm. "Let's begin by deciphering the anatomy of an RFP. It's the gateway to every government contract, and understanding it is crucial."

As William opened the folder, laying out documents and guidelines on the break room table, Sophia's determination surged anew. Here, in the humble confines of the break room, began her crash course in the intricacies of Requests for Proposals—a fundamental step toward unlocking the secrets of winning government contracts.

Their partnership had commenced, and the journey toward mastering the labyrinthine world of government procurement had officially begun.

SCENE 2

SOPHIA SAT AT her desk, poring over the papers strewn across its surface. The afternoon sun cast elongated shadows across the room, signaling the passage of time. Her concentration was unwavering as she delved into the intricacies of the RFP documents that William had left with her earlier.

A soft knock on the partially open door interrupted her focus. Without waiting for a response, Sophia's assistant, Maria, peeked in. "Sophia, sorry to disturb you. There's a courier here with a package for you."

Setting aside the RFP papers, Sophia nodded. "Please, send them in."

The courier entered, holding a nondescript package. "Delivery for Ms. Sophia Chen from the Department of Governmental Affairs," he announced, handing over the parcel.

Curiosity flickered in Sophia's eyes as she accepted the package. "Thank you. Please, have a seat for a moment."

The courier obliged, taking a chair near the desk as Sophia carefully opened the package. Inside, she found a letter and a flash drive. Her gaze flitted over the official letterhead of the Department of Governmental Affairs.

"Ms. Chen, I was instructed to deliver this personally," the courier added, observing Sophia's piqued interest. "They said it was urgent."

Sophia skimmed the letter, her brows furrowing as she read the brief message. "Thank you for bringing this. I appreciate it."

As the courier excused himself and departed, Sophia turned her attention to the flash drive, her curiosity piqued. With a quick glance around the room to ensure privacy, she inserted it into her computer, clicking through the files it contained.

To her surprise, the drive held a set of pre-solicitation documents for an upcoming government contract—precisely the kind of opportunity she and William had been discussing. It was a chance to apply the newfound knowledge, to put theory into practice.

As she sifted through the details, Sophia's heart raced with anticipation. This wasn't just any contract; it was a potential game-changer for Horizon Dynamics, an opportunity to showcase their capabilities and secure a foothold in the realm of government procurement.

Determined, Sophia made a mental note to discuss this development with William. It was a serendipitous moment—a tangible opportunity presenting itself just as they commenced their journey into government contracts.

The stage was set, the stakes higher than ever, as Sophia prepared to delve into the intricate dance of bidding and strategy. With the flash drive's contents laid bare before her, the contract conquest had taken a promising turn—one that could potentially reshape the future of Horizon Dynamics.

PART FOUR

SCENE 3

THE FAINT HUM of the projector filled the conference room as Sophia and William huddled around the table, poring over the intricate details of the upcoming government contract. Charts, graphs, and strategic notes adorned the whiteboard, mapping out their game plan.

"This contract is a significant opportunity for Horizon Dynamics," William remarked, his finger tracing the outline of a crucial timeline on the board. "But securing it won't be a walk in the park. The competition will be fierce."

Sophia nodded, her eyes fixed on the board as she absorbed William's insights. "I understand. We need to differentiate ourselves and make a compelling case for why Horizon Dynamics is the ideal choice."

"Exactly," William agreed, tapping a series of bullet points on the board. "We'll need to highlight your company's strengths, demonstrate innovation, and align with the specific needs outlined in the RFP."

As they delved deeper into the strategy, Sophia's phone buzzed with a notification. Glancing down, she noticed an email alert—a message from the Department of Governmental Affairs regarding the upcoming bidder's conference for the contract.

"William, the bidder's conference for this contract is happening next week," Sophia exclaimed, a spark of excitement igniting within her. "It's our chance to gain further insights and make connections within the agency."

"That's an excellent opportunity," William acknowledged, adjusting his glasses as he considered the information. "Attending the conference will give us a better understanding of the agency's expectations and possibly a chance to network with key decision-makers."

With a renewed sense of purpose, Sophia and William began outlining their approach for the bidder's conference. They discussed strategies to engage with agency representatives, craft compelling inquiries, and subtly showcase Horizon Dynamics' capabilities without revealing too much.

Hours passed in the conference room, the atmosphere charged with anticipation and strategic fervor. By the time Sophia glanced at the clock, the afternoon had transitioned into evening, yet their fervent planning continued.

"Tomorrow, we'll fine-tune our presentation and discussion points for the conference," William suggested, gathering their notes and materials. "It's crucial to make a strong impression and establish Horizon Dynamics as a serious contender."

Sophia nodded in agreement, a sense of determination pulsating within her. This bid was more than an opportunity; it was a pivotal moment for her company's resurgence.

As they gathered their belongings and prepared to leave, Sophia couldn't help but feel a surge of optimism. The bidder's conference awaited—a pivotal step in their quest for the elusive government contract that could redefine Horizon Dynamics' trajectory.

The stage was set for their presence at the conference—a chance to make their mark and inch closer to securing the contract that might just save her company.

SCENE 4

THE MORNING OF the bidder's conference dawned with an air of anticipation at Horizon Dynamics' office. Sophia arrived early, dressed in a tailored navy suit that exuded professionalism and confidence. William, equally prepared, greeted her with a reassuring smile as they made their way to the conference venue.

The foyer buzzed with activity as representatives from various companies gathered, all vying for the chance to secure the coveted government contract. Sophia and William navigated through the crowd, their steps purposeful, their demeanor composed.

"Remember, Sophia," William whispered, "our goal is to gather insights while subtly showcasing Horizon Dynamics' capabilities. Engage, inquire, but avoid revealing too much prematurely."

Sophia nodded, her eyes scanning the room for familiar faces. Amidst the sea of attendees, she spotted familiar logos and names of competing companies, a stark reminder of the fierce competition they faced.

The conference hall echoed with discussions and presentations. Booths and displays adorned the room, each company striving to make an impression. Sophia and William strategically made their way from booth to booth, engaging in conversations, asking pertinent questions, and keenly observing the nuances of each interaction.

At one booth, an animated discussion about innovative technology caught Sophia's attention. She exchanged ideas with the company representatives, subtly highlighting Horizon Dynamics' expertise in a similar realm without giving away proprietary details.

Moving to another corner of the hall, Sophia found herself in a conversation with a representative from a government agency, discussing the contract's specifications. Her queries were strategic, seeking clarity while subtly showcasing Horizon Dynamics' alignment with the agency's needs.

Meanwhile, William networked with other attendees, exchanging pleasantries and gathering tidbits of information that could prove valuable in their bid strategy. His years of experience shone through as he effortlessly navigated conversations, subtly advocating for Horizon Dynamics without overtly pushing their agenda.

As the conference progressed, Sophia and William remained attuned to every detail, every word exchanged, and every connection made. They seized the opportunity to gather vital insights, refine their strategy, and position Horizon Dynamics as a credible contender in the eyes of the agency representatives.

Amidst the hustle and bustle of the event, Sophia felt a sense of accomplishment. The bidder's conference had served as a crucial stepping stone, providing invaluable knowledge and establishing Horizon Dynamics as a serious player in the race for the government contract.

With a trove of newfound information and contacts, Sophia and William departed the conference, their minds already at work, strategizing the next steps in their pursuit of the elusive contract.

SCENE 5

IN THE QUIET confines of Horizon Dynamics' office, Sophia and William reconvened after the bidder's conference, their minds abuzz with the wealth of information gathered.

Sophia flipped through her notes, the pages filled with scribbles and highlighted sections from their interactions at the conference. "The insights we gained today are invaluable," she remarked, her voice carrying a mix of satisfaction and determination.

William nodded in agreement, sorting through business cards and contact information collected during their networking endeavors. "We've established connections, understood the agency's priorities, and gathered insights into our competitors' approaches."

Sophia's phone chimed with an email notification, drawing her attention. "It's an update from the Department of Governmental Affairs regarding the contract timeline," she announced, quickly scanning the contents. "They're expediting the proposal submission deadline by two weeks."

William raised an eyebrow in surprise. "That accelerates our timeline significantly. We'll need to refine our proposal strategy and ensure everything aligns within the revised timeframe."

Their conversation delved into rapid-fire brainstorming sessions, ideas bouncing back and forth as they strategized the adjustments needed to meet the accelerated deadline. They discussed refining their proposal, enhancing their value proposition, and leveraging the insights gained from the conference to strengthen their bid.

As the discussion intensified, Sophia's phone buzzed again, this time with a call from Maria, her assistant. "Excuse me for a moment, William," she said, stepping away to take the call.

Returning moments later, Sophia wore a thoughtful expression. "That was Maria. She received a call from an unknown number claiming to have information related to our bid strategy."

William's brow furrowed. "Unknown number? Did they say anything specific?"

Sophia recounted the conversation. "They mentioned having insights that could give us an edge in the bid. They want to meet in person to discuss further."

William regarded the information with caution. "It could be a strategic move by a competitor or someone with ulterior motives."

Sophia nodded in agreement. "Agreed. We need to approach this cautiously, but it could also be an opportunity to gain valuable information."

They deliberated on the situation, weighing the risks and potential gains. Sophia mulled over the decision, contemplating the possibilities of gaining an advantage versus the risks of potential manipulation or misinformation.

With a sense of cautious curiosity, Sophia made a decision. "Let's meet them, but discreetly. We need to tread carefully and validate the authenticity of their information before divulging anything crucial."

Their discussion shifted gears, evolving into plans for the upcoming meeting and strategies to safeguard Horizon Dynamics' bid secrets while potentially leveraging the offered insights.

As the day drew to a close, Sophia and William departed, their minds buzzing with the intricacies of bid strategy, the accelerating timeline, and the intriguing prospect of the upcoming clandestine meeting.

The stakes had intensified, and the journey toward winning the government contract had taken an unexpected turn—a clandestine rendezvous promising either a pivotal advantage or a perilous trap.

PART FIVE

SCENE 6

A DISCREET COFFEE shop on the outskirts of the city served as the rendezvous point for Sophia and William. The ambiance was hushed, with a few patrons engrossed in quiet conversations, providing an ideal setting for their clandestine meeting.

Sophia and William occupied a secluded corner, their demeanor cautious yet determined. The faint aroma of freshly brewed coffee mingled with an air of suspense as they awaited the unknown informant.

Minutes ticked by, and anticipation hung heavy in the air until a figure approached their table—a man in a nondescript suit, his features obscured by the dim lighting.

"Ms. Chen, Mr. Hayes," the man began in a low, measured tone, taking a seat opposite them. "I appreciate your willingness to meet."

Sophia studied the man, her instincts on high alert. "You claimed to have information relevant to our bid strategy. What can you tell us?"

The man leaned forward slightly, his voice lowered to a confidential tone. "I have insights into a competitor's approach, specifics that could give you an edge. In exchange, I seek a token of appreciation for my assistance."

Sophia exchanged a glance with William, a sense of skepticism flickering in their eyes. "And how do we know this information is genuine and not a ploy to manipulate our bid?"

The man produced a dossier from his briefcase, sliding it across the table. "You'll find details here that will corroborate the legitimacy of the information. Consider it a gesture of good faith."

Sophia hesitated, weighing the risks against the potential gains. With caution, she opened the dossier and began reviewing its contents, each page filled with intricate details regarding a competitor's proposed strategy—information that could indeed provide a strategic advantage.

"This is detailed," William noted, his gaze scanning the documents. "If authentic, it could indeed bolster our bid strategy."

The man observed their reactions, a hint of assurance in his demeanor. "Consider it an opportunity to outmaneuver your competition. I trust you'll find my assistance invaluable."

Sophia closed the dossier, her mind racing with possibilities and the need for caution. "We'll consider this information. But know that we'll verify its authenticity before making any decisions."

The man nodded, rising from the table. "Of course. I'll await your response."

As he departed, Sophia and William exchanged a knowing glance, a silent agreement passing between them. The information presented was tantalizing, but caution dictated a thorough validation process before integrating it into their bid strategy.

"We need to verify the credibility of this information discreetly," Sophia remarked, tucking the dossier into her bag. "We can't afford to take risks, especially with so much at stake."

William nodded in agreement. "Agreed. We'll employ our resources to ensure its authenticity without exposing our bid strategy."

Their conversation transitioned into plans for the verification process, discussing methods to authenticate the information while safeguarding Horizon Dynamics' bid secrets.

Leaving the coffee shop, Sophia and William carried with them a sense of cautious optimism. The information presented held promise, but its credibility remained to be confirmed—a pivotal step in their quest for the government contract.

The stage was set for the verification process—a delicate yet crucial endeavor that could potentially shift the tides in Horizon Dynamics' favor or uncover an elaborate ruse.

SCENE 7

DAYS PASSED, AND Horizon Dynamics' office hummed with activity as Sophia and William delved into the meticulous process of verifying the information obtained during the clandestine meeting. They had engaged discreet experts and conducted thorough analyses to validate the authenticity of the dossier's contents.

In Sophia's office, William sat across from her, a laptop displaying a series of reports and analyses on the table between them. "The analysis is conclusive," he stated, his tone carrying a mix of reservation and validation. "The information aligns remarkably well with industry trends and known patterns of our competitor's strategies."

Sophia nodded, her brow furrowed in contemplation. "If this information is accurate, it could indeed provide us with a substantial advantage in our bid strategy."

Their conversation halted momentarily as Maria entered the room, a sense of urgency etched on her face. "Sophia, I just received a call from an anonymous source claiming the leaked information might be a setup. They warned us to be cautious, stating it could be a ploy by a competitor to mislead our bid strategy."

Sophia exchanged a glance with William, a surge of apprehension washing over them. "Did they provide any evidence or further details?"

Maria hesitated, her voice tinged with concern. "No, it was brief, and they didn't reveal much. They insisted we be cautious and not act solely based on the information received."

Sophia's mind raced with conflicting thoughts. The verification process had seemed convincing, but the anonymous warning introduced a new layer of doubt. She pondered the potential risks of trusting the information against the consequences of dismissing it if it proved genuine.

"We need to reevaluate our approach," William suggested, his demeanor reflective. "We can't afford to proceed blindly, especially with such uncertainties."

Sophia nodded in agreement, her decision firming up. "We'll proceed cautiously. Let's prepare two bid strategies—one incorporating the information and another without it. That way, we're prepared for either scenario."

As they commenced revising their bid strategies, Sophia couldn't shake the lingering sense of uncertainty. The warning had cast doubt on the credibility of the information they had worked so diligently to validate.

With a sense of caution, Sophia and William refined their bid plans, meticulously crafting strategies that accounted for both the potential advantages and risks associated with the contested information.

The day waned into evening as Sophia sat at her desk, reviewing the revised bid strategies. Each plan meticulously detailed, each decision weighed with care and consideration.

The looming deadline added pressure, the accelerated timeline leaving little room for indecision or hesitation. The uncertainty gnawed at Sophia's resolve, prompting her to reevaluate their next steps in the pursuit of the government contract.

The stage was set for a critical decision—an intricate balance between seizing potential advantages and mitigating the risks, all in the quest for Horizon Dynamics to emerge victorious in the fiercely competitive bidding process.

SCENE 8

IN THE DIMLY lit conference room of Horizon Dynamics, Sophia and William sat, the weight of their decisions palpable in the air. On the table lay two meticulously crafted bid strategies—each representing a divergent path that could potentially shape the fate of Horizon Dynamics' bid for the government contract.

Sophia's gaze lingered on the documents, her mind navigating the intricate web of uncertainties and possibilities. The warning about the contested information continued to cast a shadow of doubt, challenging the very foundation of their bid strategy.

"We've prepared two strategies," William began, his voice reflecting the gravity of the moment. "One integrates the contested information, leveraging its potential advantages, while the other proceeds without relying on it, prioritizing caution over possible risks."

Sophia contemplated the strategies before her, each representing a distinct approach fraught with implications. "The risk of relying on potentially misleading information is substantial, yet so is the potential gain if it's authentic," she mused aloud.

William nodded in agreement, his gaze fixed on the documents. "Agreed. Our decision could determine Horizon Dynamics' trajectory, and we must tread cautiously."

A moment of contemplative silence enveloped the room as they grappled with the pivotal choice before them. The accelerated timeline added urgency, leaving little room for prolonged deliberation.

"I'm inclined to proceed with caution," Sophia finally voiced, her tone measured yet resolute. "The anonymous warning weighs heavily on my mind. We cannot afford to risk our bid strategy based solely on uncertain information."

William nodded in understanding, acknowledging the weight of Sophia's words. "Caution might be our best course of action. It's essential to prioritize a solid, reliable bid strategy over potential risks."

Their decision made, Sophia gathered the bid strategy that veered away from the contested information. With purposeful deliberation, she finalized the documents, refining their bid to align with the strategy rooted in prudence and reliability.

As the clock ticked, the moment to submit their bid drew closer. Sophia and William synchronized their efforts, ensuring the finalized strategy was comprehensive, compelling, and reflective of Horizon Dynamics' strengths without relying on uncertain details.

With the revised bid strategy in hand, Sophia felt a blend of apprehension and conviction. Their decision might forego the lure of potential advantage, but it was a choice rooted in safeguarding the integrity of their bid.

"We're ready," Sophia announced, her voice tinged with a hint of resolve. "Let's submit our bid following the strategy prioritizing caution."

William nodded in agreement, his expression mirroring Sophia's determination. "Agreed. It's time to set our course and await the outcome."

With a sense of finality, they sealed the bid package and prepared for submission, their minds focused on the future—a future shaped by their carefully considered decision in the relentless pursuit of the government contract.

The stage was set—the bid submitted, their fate now entwined with the decision to prioritize prudence over potential risks in the tumultuous world of government procurement.

PART SIX

SCENE 9

DAYS TURNED INTO a nerve-wracking wait for Sophia and William as Horizon Dynamics awaited the outcome of their bid submission. The office buzzed with an air of anticipation, each passing moment carrying the weight of uncertainty and hope.

In Sophia's office, she sat at her desk, her gaze flickering between the phone and the clock, willing it to ring with news of the bid evaluation. William paced nearby, his demeanor reflective of the tension pervading the room.

"It's nerve-wracking, waiting for their decision," William remarked, his voice tinged with a hint of restlessness.

Sophia nodded in agreement, her mind consumed with thoughts of the bid, its intricacies, and the pivotal decision to prioritize caution. "The wait feels interminable. I can't shake off the uncertainty."

Before they could dwell further on their predicament, a soft chime signaled an incoming call on Sophia's phone. With a racing heart, she answered, her voice steady despite the anticipation.

"Ms. Chen, this is Nathan Reynolds from the Department of Governmental Affairs. I'm pleased to inform you that Horizon Dynamics' bid has been evaluated positively," the voice on the other end announced, eliciting a surge of relief within Sophia.

William's eyes widened in elation as Sophia's grip tightened on the phone. "That's fantastic news, Mr. Reynolds! Thank you for informing us. We're honored and eager to move forward."

Nathan Reynolds continued, "Your proposal demonstrated innovation, alignment with our needs, and a thorough understanding of the project scope. We'd like to invite you for a final round of discussions before awarding the contract."

Sophia's heart soared with validation. "Absolutely, we're ready to discuss further details. Thank you for this opportunity."

As she hung up, a sense of exhilaration filled the room. William smiled in satisfaction, his eyes reflecting their triumph. "Congratulations, Sophia. This is a testament to our strategy paying off."

Sophia reciprocated the smile, a wave of relief washing over her. "Thank you, William. This is a pivotal moment for Horizon Dynamics."

Their victory, however, was tinged with the knowledge that the final round of discussions would determine the contract's actual award. The elation was coupled with a renewed focus on preparation and ensuring they left an indelible impression during the upcoming discussions.

"We need to prepare diligently," Sophia stated, her mind already racing with plans and strategies for the final round. "This is our chance to seal the deal and secure the contract."

William nodded in agreement, his determination mirroring Sophia's. "Indeed. Let's ensure we leave no stone unturned in presenting Horizon Dynamics as the ideal choice for this project."

With the sense of accomplishment mingled with renewed vigor, Sophia and William embarked on preparations for the final discussions—a crucial step in solidifying Horizon Dynamics' success in winning the coveted government contract.

The stage was set for the final round—a chance for Horizon Dynamics to shine, to showcase their capabilities, and to clinch the contract that could pave the way for a new chapter of success.

SCENE 10

THE DAY OF the final discussions arrived, shrouded in a mix of excitement and nervous anticipation at Horizon Dynamics. Sophia and William meticulously prepared for the meeting, their determination to leave an indelible impression evident in every detail.

In a sleek conference room adorned with Horizon Dynamics' presentations and a polished setup, Sophia and William awaited the arrival of the panel from the Department of Governmental Affairs. Each passing moment felt charged with significance, the air heavy with the weight of their ambitions.

As the designated time approached, the door swung open, and Nathan Reynolds entered with two other officials—a woman and a man—representing the agency. They exchanged cordial greetings, setting the tone for the critical discussions that would shape the contract's fate.

"Ms. Chen, Mr. Hayes, thank you for joining us," Nathan Reynolds greeted, his demeanor affable yet businesslike. "Your proposal impressed us, and we're eager to delve deeper into the specifics."

Sophia and William reciprocated the pleasantries, their confidence underpinned by thorough preparation and conviction in Horizon Dynamics' capabilities.

The discussions commenced, each slide, statistic, and narrative presented with meticulous precision. Sophia adeptly navigated through the intricacies of Horizon Dynamics' proposal, elucidating their innovative approach, alignment with the agency's requirements, and the company's steadfast commitment to excellence.

William seamlessly supplemented her presentation, providing technical insights and strategic perspectives that underscored Horizon Dynamics' strengths and unique value proposition.

As the presentations transitioned into discussions, Sophia and William engaged in a dynamic exchange with the panel, addressing queries, elaborating on key points, and deftly navigating through intricacies with confidence and expertise.

The atmosphere in the room hummed with intellectual fervor, each participant deeply engrossed in the exchange, seeking clarity, probing for insights, and assessing the potential collaboration.

With every eloquent argument, every nuanced explanation, Sophia and William painted a compelling narrative—a narrative that depicted Horizon Dynamics as not just a contender but as the ideal partner for the agency's envisioned project.

The discussions concluded with a palpable sense of accomplishment. The panel departed, their expressions betraying a mixture of intrigue and satisfaction, leaving Sophia and William with a lingering sense of optimism.

"That went well," William remarked, his voice laced with satisfaction.

Sophia nodded in agreement, a blend of relief and anticipation evident in her demeanor. "It did. Now, we await their decision."

The minutes stretched into an agonizing wait as Sophia and William held onto the hope of securing the contract that would mark a turning point for Horizon Dynamics—a culmination of their meticulous efforts, strategic acumen, and unwavering determination.

The room bore witness to their shared anticipation—the precipice between uncertainty and the tantalizing prospect of success in Horizon Dynamics' quest for the prestigious government contract.

SCENE 11

DAYS STRETCHED INTO an interminable wait for Sophia and William, each passing moment weighed down by the anticipation of the final decision from the Department of Governmental Affairs. At Horizon Dynamics' office, the atmosphere teetered between hope and apprehension.

In Sophia's office, she sat at her desk, her gaze fixed on the phone, willing it to ring with news of the contract decision. William, nearby, attempted to mask his restlessness with a veneer of calm, though the tension in the room was palpable.

A soft chime signaled an incoming email. Sophia's heart skipped a beat as she hastily checked her inbox. The subject line read: "Notification of Contract Award."

With bated breath, Sophia opened the email, her eyes scanning the contents fervently. Her expression morphed from anticipation to elation as she absorbed the message—a surge of joy and relief enveloping her.

"It's here, William," she exclaimed, unable to contain her excitement. "We've been awarded the contract!"

William's eyes widened in sheer delight as a grin spread across his face. "That's incredible news, Sophia! Congratulations!"

Their shared jubilation filled the room, a sense of accomplishment washing over them. The realization that their efforts had borne fruit, that Horizon Dynamics had clinched the coveted government contract, was nothing short of a triumphant moment.

Sophia composed herself and quickly replied to confirm their acceptance of the contract terms, expressing gratitude and eagerness to embark on the project.

As the email sent, she leaned back in her chair, a mix of emotions coursing through her. "This is a game-changer for Horizon Dynamics," she remarked, her voice tinged with a sense of triumph.

William nodded in agreement, his excitement barely contained. "Absolutely. This contract opens up a new chapter for our company."

Their victory was not just a personal triumph; it signified a significant milestone for Horizon Dynamics—a testament to their perseverance, strategic acumen, and unwavering commitment to success in the realm of government contracts.

Amidst the jubilation, plans and discussions for the project's initiation were already underway. Sophia and William prepared to assemble the team, align resources, and commence the transformative work outlined in the contract.

The energy in the office was electric, each member of the Horizon Dynamics team sharing in the celebration and eagerly gearing up for the promising journey ahead.

As the day drew to a close, Sophia reflected on the journey—the challenges faced, the strategic maneuvers made, and the ultimate triumph. The road to securing the government contract had been arduous, but it marked a pivotal victory for Horizon Dynamics, solidifying its position in the competitive landscape of government procurement.

The stage was set for a new phase—an era of opportunity, growth, and accomplishments for Horizon Dynamics, all stemming from the success in winning the transformative government contract.

PART SEVEN

SCENE 12

THE MORNING AFTER the contract award buzzed with heightened energy at Horizon Dynamics. Sophia arrived early, her steps brimming with purpose and determination. The office was abuzz with excitement, the air charged with anticipation for the new project's commencement.

In the conference room, Sophia and William gathered with key team members, their faces reflecting a mix of eagerness and resolve. The table was adorned with project briefs, timelines, and strategic plans—an embodiment of the company's readiness to embark on the transformative venture.

"Good morning, everyone," Sophia greeted, her voice carrying an aura of enthusiasm. "Today marks the beginning of an exciting journey for Horizon Dynamics. Our hard work has paid off, and now it's time to deliver on our commitment."

The team echoed her sentiment, their collective enthusiasm palpable. Each member was attuned to the significance of the moment—the opportunity to showcase their expertise, contribute to a groundbreaking project, and further solidify Horizon Dynamics' reputation.

Sophia initiated the meeting, outlining the project's objectives, deliverables, and the strategic direction for seamless execution. She emphasized the importance of synergy, collaboration, and maintaining the high standards that had earned them the contract.

"As we embark on this project, let's leverage our strengths," Sophia urged, her eyes meeting each team member's gaze. "Our success depends on seamless teamwork, innovation, and an unwavering commitment to excellence."

William supplemented her remarks, providing insights into the project's technical aspects and strategic alignment. His guidance underscored the importance of meticulous planning and the need for each team member's dedication to the project's success.

The meeting progressed into discussions, brainstorming sessions, and the delineation of responsibilities. Each team member contributed ideas, raised pertinent questions, and enthusiastically engaged in charting the course for the project's successful execution.

As the discussions intensified, a sense of camaraderie and shared purpose permeated the room. The team synergized, leveraging their collective expertise, and refining strategies to address potential challenges that lay ahead.

Sophia interjected with a final rallying call, "Let's set the bar high for this project. Our goal is not just to meet expectations but to exceed them. Together, we'll showcase Horizon Dynamics' capabilities and deliver exceptional results."

With a sense of determination, the meeting concluded, the team members dispersing to their respective roles and tasks, energized and eager to embark on the new project.

As Sophia watched her team depart, a surge of pride and optimism filled her. The collective commitment and enthusiasm displayed during the meeting affirmed Horizon Dynamics' potential to excel in delivering on the contract's promises.

The journey had only just begun—a journey that promised challenges, innovation, and the opportunity to demonstrate Horizon Dynamics' prowess in a transformative project that could reshape the company's trajectory in government contracting.

SCENE 13

DAYS MELDED INTO a whirlwind of activity at Horizon Dynamics as the team dove headfirst into the project, each member meticulously fulfilling their roles and responsibilities. Sophia oversaw the operations, ensuring the project's trajectory aligned with the established timeline and quality benchmarks.

In Sophia's office, she reviewed progress reports and timelines, her focus unwavering as she delved into the project's intricacies. The phone rang, interrupting her concentration.

"Ms. Chen, it's Nathan Reynolds from the Department of Governmental Affairs," the voice on the other end announced.

Sophia's heart quickened at the unexpected call. "Mr. Reynolds, good morning. How may I assist you?"

"I wanted to touch base regarding the project's progress," Nathan began. "We've been impressed with Horizon Dynamics' commitment and the initial strides made. However, there's an unforeseen challenge that has arisen."

Sophia listened intently, her mind swiftly assessing the situation. "Please, go on."

Nathan explained the challenge—a shift in the project's scope due to evolving regulatory requirements. The agency sought Horizon Dynamics' flexibility and innovative approach to adapt to these changes while ensuring project success.

"I understand the gravity of the situation, Mr. Reynolds," Sophia replied, her voice composed yet resolute. "We're committed to delivering as per the updated scope. I'll convene our team immediately to devise a strategy that aligns with the revised requirements."

With the call ended, Sophia's thoughts raced. She swiftly gathered her team, articulating the new challenge and emphasizing the need for innovative solutions to address the revised project scope.

In the conference room, the team assembled, their faces reflecting a blend of determination and anticipation. Sophia outlined the situation, emphasizing the importance of adaptability and creative problem-solving in navigating the altered project landscape.

"Team, our adaptability defines our strength," Sophia asserted, her tone imbued with confidence. "Let's harness our expertise and collaborative spirit to devise a strategy that not only meets but exceeds the updated requirements."

The team engaged in vibrant discussions, brainstorming sessions, and rigorous analysis. Ideas flowed freely, each member contributing their unique perspectives and expertise to chart a path forward.

As the discussions progressed, a sense of camaraderie and focused determination enveloped the room. The team synergized, exploring innovative approaches and refining strategies that aligned with the revised project scope.

Through collaborative efforts and creative problem-solving, they began formulating a comprehensive plan that not only addressed the challenge but also showcased Horizon Dynamics' adaptability and commitment to delivering exceptional results.

With the meeting concluded, the team dispersed, invigorated by the shared determination to navigate the unforeseen challenge and deliver a solution that would uphold Horizon Dynamics' reputation for excellence.

Sophia remained in the conference room, her mind consumed with possibilities and strategies to overcome the hurdle. She was acutely aware that the successful resolution of this challenge would not only solidify Horizon Dynamics' capabilities but also strengthen their relationship with the Department of Governmental Affairs.

The unexpected twist had presented an opportunity—a chance for Horizon Dynamics to showcase their adaptability, innovation, and resilience in the face of adversity.

SCENE 14

IN THE DAYS that followed the team meeting, Horizon Dynamics' office buzzed with intensified activity. Sophia and her team worked tirelessly, implementing the strategies devised to navigate the unexpected challenge posed by the revised project scope.

Sophia found herself engrossed in numerous discussions, analysis reports, and strategy sessions. Her office became a hub of focused activity as she collaborated closely with key team members, ensuring the seamless execution of the adapted plan.

Amidst the organized chaos, William entered her office, a look of urgency etched on his face. "Sophia, I've received an urgent update from the Department of Governmental Affairs," he announced, his voice tinged with concern.

Sophia's attention instantly shifted to him. "What's the update, William?"

"They've expressed concerns about the timeline for adapting to the revised scope," William explained, handing over a document outlining the agency's apprehensions. "They're seeking reassurance that we can accommodate the changes within the stipulated timeframe."

Sophia scanned through the document, a sense of determination settling over her. "We anticipated this challenge, and we're well on our way to addressing it," she reassured, her voice steady despite the growing pressure.

William nodded in agreement, his confidence unwavering. "Indeed, our team has been working around the clock to ensure we meet the revised requirements."

With a resolute nod, Sophia picked up the phone, initiating a call to Nathan Reynolds. The conversation centered on assuring the agency of Horizon Dynamics' dedication, the progress made in adapting to the new scope, and the measures in place to meet the revised timeline.

"Mr. Reynolds, I want to reassure you that we're fully committed to delivering as per the revised scope," Sophia conveyed earnestly. "We've allocated additional resources and implemented innovative strategies to ensure the project's success."

After a thorough discussion, Sophia concluded the call, a mix of relief and determination evident in her expression. "We're on track, William. But we need to escalate our efforts further to allay their concerns completely."

William nodded, his demeanor reflective of their shared determination. "Agreed. We'll intensify our efforts and keep them updated on our progress."

The days that ensued saw Horizon Dynamics' team working with renewed vigor, the sense of urgency propelling them to surpass expectations. Collaborative efforts, late nights, and relentless dedication characterized their pursuit to meet the revised project scope within the stringent timeline.

As the deadline approached, the team's commitment and hard work bore fruit. They achieved significant milestones, successfully aligning the project's deliverables with the updated requirements.

With each hurdle overcome, each challenge surmounted, Horizon Dynamics solidified its reputation for adaptability, resilience, and unwavering dedication to excellence in government projects.

The successful adaptation to the revised scope marked a pivotal moment—a testament to Horizon Dynamics' ability to thrive even in the face of unexpected challenges.

PART EIGHT

SCENE 15

THE SUCCESS OF Horizon Dynamics' adaptation to the revised project scope echoed through the company's corridors. The atmosphere in the office was buoyant, team members filled with a sense of accomplishment, having successfully navigated the unexpected challenge and strengthened their partnership with the Department of Governmental Affairs.

In Sophia's office, she sat reviewing the latest progress reports, satisfaction evident in her expression. The phone chimed, indicating an incoming call. She answered, expecting updates related to the project.

"Ms. Chen, it's Nathan Reynolds," came the familiar voice on the line.

"Nathan, good to hear from you," Sophia greeted warmly. "How can I assist you today?"

"I wanted to extend my appreciation for the remarkable effort your team put forth to accommodate the changes," Nathan expressed, his tone carrying a hint of admiration. "Your dedication hasn't gone unnoticed."

Sophia smiled, grateful for the recognition. "Thank you, Nathan. We're committed to delivering excellence in every aspect of our partnership."

"I'm calling with some positive news," Nathan continued, a note of enthusiasm in his voice. "Based on the impressive progress and your team's adaptability, the agency is considering expanding the project scope. We're impressed with Horizon Dynamics' capabilities and would like to explore additional areas where your expertise could be invaluable."

Sophia's heart quickened with the revelation. The prospect of an expanded project signaled not only recognition of their competence but also the potential for further collaboration and growth.

"We're excited about the opportunity, Nathan," Sophia replied, her voice tinged with excitement. "We're ready to discuss and contribute to any new areas that align with our expertise."

As the call concluded, Sophia's mind buzzed with possibilities. The potential expansion meant not just a new phase in the ongoing project but also an opportunity to showcase Horizon Dynamics' versatility and establish a more profound relationship with the agency.

Sophia wasted no time; she summoned her core team for an impromptu meeting. The news of potential expansion filled the room with renewed excitement and a sense of purpose.

"Team, our hard work has opened new doors for us," Sophia announced, her voice charged with enthusiasm. "The agency is considering expanding the project scope, seeking our expertise in additional areas."

The team erupted into animated discussions, ideas flying across the room, and strategies forming on how best to approach the potential expansion. Each member brought forth their insights and suggestions, their enthusiasm a testament to their dedication and ambition.

With a newfound sense of purpose, the team embarked on drafting a proposal outlining Horizon Dynamics' capabilities in the prospective areas, underscoring their commitment to delivering excellence in any new endeavor.

The prospect of an expanded scope invigorated the office, igniting a collective drive to seize this opportunity and further solidify Horizon Dynamics' position as a frontrunner in government contracting.

The scene was set for a new chapter—a chance for Horizon Dynamics to broaden its horizons, leverage its expertise, and cement its reputation for unparalleled excellence in government projects.

SCENE 16

DAYS TURNED INTO weeks as Horizon Dynamics' team meticulously crafted the proposal for the potential expansion. The office was a hive of focused activity, team members engrossed in research, analysis, and strategy sessions to outline the company's capabilities in the prospective areas.

In Sophia's office, she reviewed the draft proposal, meticulously ensuring it encapsulated Horizon Dynamics' strengths, expertise, and innovative approach. The phone rang, interrupting her concentration.

"Sophia, it's William," came the urgent voice on the line.

Sophia sensed the urgency in his tone. "William, what's the matter?"

"The agency wants an immediate meeting to discuss our proposal for the expansion," William relayed, his voice filled with a sense of urgency. "They're eager to explore our ideas further."

Sophia swiftly organized a meeting, summoning the key members involved in crafting the proposal. As they gathered, anticipation hung in the air, the team ready to present their comprehensive plan to the agency.

In the conference room, Sophia and her team sat across from representatives of the Department of Governmental Affairs—a moment pregnant with anticipation and possibility.

"Thank you for this opportunity," Sophia began, her tone confident yet amiable. "We've worked diligently on a proposal outlining Horizon Dynamics' capabilities for the potential expansion."

She launched into the presentation, eloquently articulating the company's expertise, innovative strategies, and proposed methodologies for the new areas. Each team member seamlessly supplemented her presentation with their insights and contributions, highlighting Horizon Dynamics' readiness to embark on these new challenges.

As the presentation concluded, Nathan Reynolds, representing the agency, nodded thoughtfully. "This is impressive. Your proposal exhibits foresight, innovation, and aligns well with our agency's goals."

He paused, surveying the team. "We're highly intrigued by the potential of this expanded collaboration. Horizon Dynamics has showcased a remarkable ability to adapt and excel."

Sophia felt a surge of anticipation and pride. The agency's positive reception of their proposal was a testament to their hard work and dedication.

"We're excited about the prospect of working together on this expanded initiative," Nathan continued, a hint of enthusiasm in his voice. "Let's proceed with the next steps to formalize the expanded scope of our collaboration."

The room erupted in quiet celebration and nods of agreement as the team and agency representatives discussed the roadmap ahead—negotiating terms, outlining project milestones, and formalizing the expanded scope of Horizon Dynamics' involvement.

With the meeting concluded, a sense of accomplishment pervaded the room. The potential expansion marked not just a new phase in the partnership but also a validation of Horizon Dynamics' capabilities, solidifying the company's position as a trusted partner in governmental projects.

The stage was set for Horizon Dynamics to venture into new territories, leveraging their expertise and innovative approach to contribute significantly to the agency's endeavors.

SCENE 17

FOLLOWING THE SUCCESSFUL meeting with the Department of Governmental Affairs, Horizon Dynamics found itself on the brink of a significant milestone—the commencement of the expanded project. The office thrummed with a sense of anticipation and readiness to embark on this new phase of collaboration.

In Sophia's office, she sat with William, poring over the finalized agreement and project timeline. They were engrossed in strategic discussions, ensuring every detail aligned with Horizon Dynamics' commitment to excellence.

The phone buzzed, interrupting their conversation. Sophia picked up, recognizing Nathan Reynolds' number.

"Nathan, good to hear from you," she greeted, a note of excitement in her voice.

"Sophia, I wanted to inform you that the formalities for the expanded project have been completed," Nathan relayed, his tone conveying satisfaction. "The agency is eagerly looking forward to commencing work with Horizon Dynamics."

Sophia's heart swelled with pride and anticipation. "That's fantastic news, Nathan. We're equally excited about this collaboration."

As the call concluded, Sophia turned to William, a smile playing on her lips. "It's official. We're ready to dive into the expanded project."

William mirrored her smile, his eyes reflecting their shared sense of accomplishment. "This is a testament to the team's hard work and dedication."

Their discussion shifted to the next steps—mobilizing resources, assembling the project team, and orchestrating the initial phases of the expanded initiative.

Days melded into weeks as Horizon Dynamics' office buzzed with fervent activity. Teams were assembled, strategies refined, and preparations meticulously executed to kickstart the expanded project on a high note.

In a boardroom filled with anticipation, Sophia led the kickoff meeting for the expanded initiative. Team members from various departments gathered, their faces brimming with enthusiasm and determination.

"Today marks a significant milestone for Horizon Dynamics," Sophia began, her voice resonating with pride. "We're embarking on a new phase of collaboration with the Department of Governmental Affairs, leveraging our expertise and innovation."

She outlined the project's vision, goals, and emphasized the importance of collective effort in delivering excellence. Each team member was tasked with specific responsibilities, fostering a sense of ownership and shared commitment to the project's success.

The room buzzed with excitement and determination as the teams dispersed, ready to delve into their roles and contribute their expertise to the expanded project.

As the day drew to a close, Sophia reflected on the journey that had brought them to this pivotal moment—the challenges overcome, the successes celebrated, and the unwavering dedication that defined Horizon Dynamics' trajectory in government contracting.

The expanded project marked not just a new venture but an opportunity to solidify the company's standing as a leader in delivering innovative solutions and excellence in governmental collaborations.

The stage was set for Horizon Dynamics to showcase its capabilities, forge deeper partnerships, and make a significant impact on governmental projects—a testament to their resilience, adaptability, and unwavering pursuit of excellence.

PART NINE

SCENE 18

MONTHS PASSED, AND the corridors of Horizon Dynamics hummed with focused activity. The expanded project had unfolded into a transformative journey, marked by innovation, collaboration, and the collective determination of the company's team.

In Sophia's office, she sat reviewing the final reports and project outcomes. The phone rang, and she answered, recognizing the number to be from the Department of Governmental Affairs.

"Nathan, it's good to hear from you," Sophia greeted warmly.

"Sophia, I wanted to express our sincere gratitude for Horizon Dynamics' outstanding contributions to the project," Nathan conveyed, genuine appreciation evident in his voice. "Your team's dedication and innovative solutions have been invaluable."

Sophia smiled, feeling a sense of fulfillment at the acknowledgment. "Thank you, Nathan. It's been a privilege to collaborate with your agency."

"As a token of our appreciation for your exceptional work," Nathan continued, "the agency has decided to extend the collaboration, offering Horizon Dynamics opportunities for future projects."

Sophia's heart swelled with pride and gratitude. "We're honored by this opportunity, Nathan. Horizon Dynamics looks forward to future collaborations."

With the call ended, Sophia leaned back in her chair, a sense of accomplishment washing over her. The recognition and extension of collaboration marked not just a success for Horizon Dynamics but also a validation of the company's capabilities and commitment to excellence.

Weeks passed, and the office buzzed with anticipation as Horizon Dynamics received news of securing additional government contracts, each project a testament to the company's expertise and unwavering dedication.

In a celebratory gathering, Sophia addressed the team, gratitude resonating in her voice. "This success belongs to each one of you. Your hard work, innovation, and collaborative spirit have elevated Horizon Dynamics to new heights."

The team erupted into applause, celebrating their collective achievements—a shared journey marked by resilience, innovation, and a commitment to excellence.

As the day drew to a close, Sophia stood by the office window, reflecting on the journey that had brought Horizon Dynamics to this triumphant moment. The company had not only secured prestigious government contracts but had also solidified its position as a trailblazer in the realm of government projects.

The story of Horizon Dynamics wasn't just about winning contracts; it was a testament to the power of teamwork, resilience, and unwavering dedication to delivering excellence.

As the sun dipped below the horizon, Sophia felt a sense of pride—a pride in the remarkable journey that had transformed Horizon Dynamics into a frontrunner in government contracting—a journey fueled by ambition, perseverance, and an unwavering commitment to success.

The horizon stretched before them—an expanse of endless opportunities, each one a testament to the company's capabilities, dedication, and the triumph of teamwork.

SCENE 19

THE CULMINATION OF Horizon Dynamics' efforts materialized into an exhilarating crescendo of success. The company had not only secured prestigious government contracts but had also redefined its standing as an industry leader in government projects.

In a vibrant conference room adorned with charts, statistics, and project summaries, the Horizon Dynamics team assembled for a celebratory meeting—a culmination of their hard work, dedication, and unwavering commitment to excellence.

Sophia, accompanied by William, stood at the head of the room, a beaming smile adorning her face as she addressed the team. "Today, we gather to celebrate our collective triumphs. The numbers, the achievements, they're a testament to each one of you."

She gestured toward the screens displaying graphs and figures showcasing Horizon Dynamics' impressive results—increased contract acquisitions by 60%, successful project completions 20% ahead of schedule, and client satisfaction ratings soaring to an all-time high of 95%.

"Our success is quantifiable, thanks to your relentless dedication," Sophia continued, her voice filled with pride. "But it's not just about the numbers; it's about the impact we've made, the innovations we've brought, and the trust we've earned."

William stepped forward, a projector displaying a map dotted with locations across the country. "Our reach has expanded. These markers represent the communities impacted by our projects—improved infrastructures, cutting-edge technologies, and advancements benefiting countless lives."

The room resonated with applause, a symphony of achievement reverberating through the walls—a testament to the remarkable journey Horizon Dynamics had undertaken.

Amidst the celebration, Nathan Reynolds, accompanied by other agency representatives, entered the room. "Congratulations, Horizon

Dynamics," he congratulated, his expression mirroring the pride felt across the room. "Your contributions have been exceptional."

Nathan handed Sophia an envelope, marked with the agency's seal. "This is a token of appreciation for your outstanding performance and commitment to excellence."

As Sophia opened the envelope, a collective hush fell over the room. Inside lay a commendation letter from the Department of Governmental Affairs—a recognition of Horizon Dynamics' unparalleled contributions, acknowledging the company as an exemplary partner in government projects.

The room erupted into cheers, applause, and heartfelt congratulations—a culmination of the company's relentless efforts and dedication.

As the celebrations ensued, Sophia looked around, her heart brimming with gratitude. The success wasn't just about contracts won; it was about the lives impacted, the communities transformed, and the indelible mark Horizon Dynamics had left on the landscape of government projects.

The horizon stretched before them—an endless expanse of opportunities earned through hard work, dedication, and a shared vision of excellence. As the cheers subsided, a resounding sense of fulfillment settled upon the Horizon Dynamics team—a testament to their unwavering commitment and the limitless possibilities ahead.

PART TEN

SEVERAL YEARS HAD passed since the vibrant celebration that marked Horizon Dynamics' triumphant achievements. The company had continued to flourish, expanding its reach, and solidifying its reputation as an industry leader in government contracting.

In a tastefully decorated office adorned with accolades and mementos of success, Sophia sat behind her desk, reflecting on the remarkable journey that had brought Horizon Dynamics to its current pinnacle.

The phone buzzed, interrupting her reverie. It was William, her trusted partner and now the Chief Operating Officer of Horizon Dynamics. "Sophia, I have exciting news," he exclaimed.

Sophia's curiosity piqued. "What's the news, William?"

"We've just secured the largest government contract in our company's history," William relayed, his voice tinged with exhilaration. "It's a testament to our continued excellence and the trust placed in us by our partners."

A smile graced Sophia's face, a mix of pride and fulfillment. "That's incredible, William. It's a testament to the dedication of our team."

As the call ended, Sophia's thoughts drifted to the team—their unwavering commitment, their innovative spirit, and their collective efforts that had propelled Horizon Dynamics to unprecedented heights.

Outside her office window, the cityscape sprawled, a reflection of the company's expansive reach—a testament to the countless communities positively impacted by Horizon Dynamics' projects.

Sophia penned a note, a token of gratitude to the team—a reminder of their shared journey, their triumphs, and the endless possibilities they had unlocked together.

The epilogue marked not just the culmination of a book but the continuation of Horizon Dynamics' story—a story defined by resilience, innovation, and an unyielding pursuit of excellence.

As Sophia leaned back in her chair, the horizon stretched before her—an endless expanse of opportunities and challenges, awaiting Horizon Dynamics' unwavering dedication and commitment to making a lasting impact in the realm of government projects.

The legacy of Horizon Dynamics was not just in the contracts secured or the accolades earned; it was in the lives transformed, the communities uplifted, and the indelible mark left on the landscape of government contracting—a legacy that would continue to thrive, guided by the company's unwavering pursuit of excellence.

The horizon beckoned—a canvas of endless possibilities—waiting for Horizon Dynamics to script the next chapter in its remarkable journey.

PART ELEVEN

MEET A DISTINGUISHED authority in government contracting and strategic business development—an individual committed to transforming businesses into powerhouses within the federal government sector. Wissem Sghaier has helped over 300 entrepreneurs and companies navigate the complexities of securing and excelling in federal contracts. His expertise has proven instrumental in propelling businesses to new heights of success. For invaluable insights and a chance to elevate your venture in the federal arena, join the Federal Government Accelerator program at https://training.fgalive.com, where expertise meets opportunity. Take the leap towards unlocking your full potential and making an impactful stride in the federal contracting domain.

www.ingramcontent.com/pod-product-compliance
Lightning Source LLC
Chambersburg PA
CBHW071215290526
45796CB00008B/250